LIGHTNING BOLT BOOKS™

How Is a Ship Like a Shark?
Vehicles Imitating Nature

Walt Brody

Lerner Publications ◆ Minneapolis

Lerner Publications Company
An imprint of Lerner Publishing Group, Inc.
241 First Avenue North
Minneapolis, MN 55401 USA

For reading levels and more information, look up this title at www.lernerbooks.com.

Main body text set in Billy Infant Regular. Typeface provided by SparkType.

Editor: Alison Lorenz **Designer:** Martha Kranes

Library of Congress Cataloging-in-Publication Data

Names: Brody, Walt, 1978– author.
Title: How is a ship like a shark? : vehicles imitating nature / Walt Brody.
Description: Minneapolis : Lerner Publications, 2022. | Series: Lightning bolt books—imitating nature | Includes bibliographical references and index. | Audience: Ages 6–9 | Audience: Grades 2–3 | Summary: "Animals have mastered motion. So why not take inspiration from them when perfecting human planes, trains, ships, cars, and more? Find out how biomimicry has influenced cutting-edge vehicle innovation" —Provided by publisher.
Identifiers: LCCN 2020003390 (print) | LCCN 2020003391 (ebook) | ISBN 9781728404165 (lib. bdg.) | ISBN 9781728418421 (eb pdf)
Subjects: LCSH: Transportation engineering—Juvenile literature. | Vehicles—Juvenile literature. | Biomimicry—Juvenile literature.
Classification: LCC TA1149 .B76 2021 (print) | LCC TA1149 (ebook) | DDC 629.04/6—dc23

LC record available at https://lccn.loc.gov/2020003390
LC ebook record available at https://lccn.loc.gov/2020003391

Manufactured in the United States of America
1-48474-48988-10/28/2020

Table of Contents

Inventions from Nature

Engineers make new things. They also try to make old things better. Good inventions make people's lives easier.

Some ideas for inventions come from nature. This is called biomimicry. *Bio* means "life," and *mimic* means "to copy."

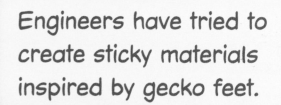

Engineers have tried to create sticky materials inspired by gecko feet.

Ships and Shark Scales

Algae and barnacles grow on the bottoms of ships. This slows the ships down. The slow ships need more fuel to move.

Barnacles

Sharks help ships save fuel. Sharkskin is made of special scales. Algae and barnacles do not grow on the scales.

Sharkskin is too sharp for algae or barnacles to grow.

Engineers designed a coating like shark scales. They put the coating on US Navy ships. They hoped it would keep algae and barnacles from growing.

When navy ships work well, they help to keep people safe.

The shark scale coating worked. The ships moved smoothly through the water and used less fuel.

Bullet Trains and Bird Beaks

Japanese bullet trains move very quickly. They can go up to 200 miles (322 km) per hour.

Bullet trains have a problem. They go so fast that they make a loud booming sound. Air rushing around the train makes the sound.

This plane rushed very quickly through a wall of air, which makes a booming sound.

A Japanese train engineer loved to watch birds. He knew the kingfisher splashes very little when it dives into water.

A kingfisher

The train's new nose keeps air from gathering around it.

He designed a new nose for the trains. He shaped them like a kingfisher's beak. The new trains move without the booming sound.

Supercars and Sailfish

McLaren Automotive makes superfast cars. The company is always trying to make them faster.

A McLaren car engineer went on vacation. He learned of a very fast fish called a sailfish.

Sailfish can swim as fast as cars go on a highway!

McLaren studied the sailfish to see what makes the fish fast. McLaren found that the fish's scales help it move quickly.

The company made a material textured like the scales. The material helped bring air into the engine. This gave the car more power. It could go even faster!

The McLaren P1 supercar

Airplanes and Bird Wings

Airbus studies birds to make its airplanes better. Some birds make small wing changes when the wind gusts. Airbus made its airplane wings change too.

Wing adjustments help planes cut through the air.

The airplane's nose senses gusts of wind. Then the wings adjust themselves. The changing wings help the airplane move more smoothly and quietly.

Many new inventions use biomimicry. Traits found in nature can make technology better.

The Future of Vehicles

Naomi Nakayama is a biologist. She studies how dandelion seeds float. The seeds have bristles on their ends. Bristles are short, stiff fibers. Nakayama found that the bristles create an air bubble around each seed. This bubble helps the seed float longer. Bubbles like these might help create new kinds of flying vehicles.

Glossary

adjust: to move or change to fit a situation

barnacle: a small living thing that grows on the bottoms of ships

biomimicry: getting ideas for inventions from nature

engineer: someone who designs vehicles or machines

fuel: what vehicles use to power their engines

gust: when the wind gets stronger for a short time

material: a type of matter such as wood, metal, or fabric

trait: a quality that makes one thing different from another

Learn More

Ducksters: Scientists and Inventors
https://www.ducksters.com/biography/scientists
/scientists_and_inventors.php

Fishman, Jon M. *Cool Sports Cars.* Minneapolis:
Lerner Publications, 2019.

Kiddle: Shark Facts for Kids
https://kids.kiddle.co/Shark

Kiddle: US Navy Facts for Kids
https://kids.kiddle.co/United_States_Navy

Rhatigan, Joe. *Wacky Inventions of the Future:
Weird Inventions That Seem Too Crazy to Be Real!*
Lake Forest, CA: Walter Foster Jr., 2019.

Waxman, Laura Hamilton. *Cool Kid Inventions.*
Minneapolis: Lerner Publications, 2020.

Index

Photo Acknowledgments

Image credits: Duangdaw/Shutterstock.com, p. 2; David Tadevosian/Shutterstock.com, p. 4; Mr.B-king/Shutterstock.com, p. 5; Maciej Mienciuk/Shutterstock.com, p. 6; Gregory S. Paulson/Getty Images, p. 7; Aliioss xeii/Shutterstock.com, p. 8; Terence Deleon Guerrero/U. S. Navy, p. 9; tackune/Shutterstock.com, p. 10; Katerina_S/Shutterstock.com, p. 11; CHENG WEI/Shutterstock.com, p. 12; Shawn.ccf/Shutterstock.com, p. 13; UM-UMM/Shutterstock.com, p. 14; wildestanimal/Shutterstock.com, p. 15; kelldallfall/Shutterstock.com, p. 16; VanderWolf Images/Shutterstock.com, p. 17; aapsky/Shutterstock.com, p. 17; Sriram Bird Photographer/Shutterstock.com, p. 18; kan_chana/Shutterstock.com, p. 20.

Cover images: Lukas Walter/Shutterstock.com; David Acosta Allely/Shutterstock.com.